DISNEP

Pooh's A-Zzzz

A B C D E

Ladybird

A is for acorn

From the top of an
oak tree, in the
Hundred-Acre
Wood.
A little acorn
fell right
where Pooh
Bear stood.

B is for bear

Some bears growl,
some bears snort.

But Pooh
Bear is the
humming sort.

C

is for carrot

Carrots are so
good to munch,
Rabbit grows them
by the bunch.

D

is for
door

In spring,
Pooh's door
is open wide

To let the
sunshine
come inside.

E

**is for
Eeyore**

Eeyore's grey.
Although
it's true,
he frequently
is a little
bit blue.

F

is for
footprint

Our footprints
always follow us
on days when
it's been
snowing.

They always
show us where
we've been,

but never
where we're going.

G

is for
gopher

'Hello!' says Gopher
to Winnie the Pooh.

'I've just come up
To visit you!'

H is for honey

'My favourite snack,'
says Winnie the
Pooh,
'is one jar of
honey...

or possibly
two!'

I
is for
ice skates

Though others give him funny glances,
On ice skates Pooh Bear
takes no
chances.

J

is for
jump

Rum-tee-tiddle-tum,
tiddle-tum-too.
When Kanga jumps,
so does Roo.

K is for kite

When the blustery Autumn breezes blow,

Up in the air kite and Piglet go!

L is for ladder

A ladder is helpful
for going up and
down trees,
When hunting
for honey
or running
from bees.

M is for mirror

'The Pooh in the
mirror is quite clever,'
says Pooh.
'He knows how to
copy whatever I do.'

N is for nose

Why do we have,
do you suppose,
two eyes,
two ears,
but just
one nose?

O

is for Owl

Owl likes to
talk a lot.
He's really quite
a bore!

He tells Pooh
everything he knows.
And sometimes
even more!

P

is for Piglet

Piglet is so
very small.
Sometimes
he can't be
seen at all!

Q is for quilt

Let it snow and
let it storm!

Under his
quilt Pooh
is cosy and
warm!

20

R

is for
Rabbit

Rabbit is so
very busy.
Watching him
makes Pooh
Bear dizzy.

21

S

is for
seesaw

Never make
a seesaw date,
with a bear
who's overweight!

T

is for
Tigger

Though
winter's here
and the birds
don't sing,

Tigger's tail
still has its
bouncy spring!

23

U is for umbrella

Clever Pooh
is now afloat

In his own
umbrella boat!

V is for vest

Piglet's vest
is warm and snug.

It fits him like
an all-day hug!

W is for woozle

There's
nothing to
fear from a
woozle
it seems.

They're only
found in
Pooh Bear's
dreams.

X is for
xylophone

Pooh's made
a honeypot
xylophone,

And, oh, it has
the sweetest tone.

Y is for yawn

Put on your nightcap, you old sleepy head!

The yawn on your face means it's time for bed!

Z is for

A sound that Pooh
makes in bed.
Begins and ends
with the letter Z.

z z z z z z z z Z Z Z Z Z Z Z Z

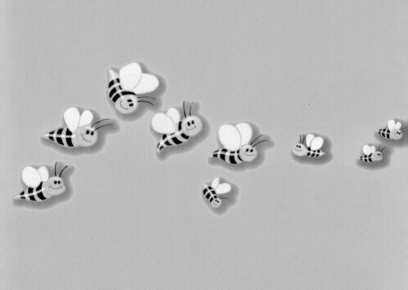